HAVE A GREAT SHIT

The Best Bathroom Book

Written & Illustrated
by Jesse Karras

Foreword by
Dr. Charles Hamori, M.D.

Text & Illustrations Copyright © 2020 by Jesse Karras

All rights reserved. No part of this publication may be reproduced, stored in a retrieval system or transmitted, in any form or by any means, electronic, mechanical, photocopying, recording, or otherwise, without prior permission, in writing, from Jesse Karras email: jesse@haveagreatshit.com

ISBN: 978-1-7344597-0-8

Cover and interior design by Jesse Karras

Disclaimer

While it is my sincere hope that you achieve optimal success in the bathroom and in your life, this book is not intended as a medical guide.

The material presented should not be construed as medical advice or instruction. No action or inaction should be taken based on the contents of this book; instead, readers should consult appropriate health professionals on any matter relating to their health and well-being.

Acknowledgements

I wish to warmly thank my family and friends
who helped make this book a reality.
I truly appreciate your enthusiasm,
encouragement, and creative input!

Chapters

1. Foreword i
2. Introduction iii
3. How to Shit 1
4. Poop School 23
5. Pain in the Ass 53
6. Going Public 67
7. Don't be a Shit 89
8. The Perfect Potty 93
9. Potty Humor 103
10. Talking Shit 109
11. Interesting Shit........................... 119

Foreword

By Dr. Charles Hamori, M.D.

When Jesse asked me to write a brief foreword for his book 'Have a Great Shit – The Best Bathroom Book' I was more than happy to do so. While the writing is both funny and pun-filled, there is little doubt that the research and approach are well-presented and informative. The book's recommendations have a good evidence base, and reflect the current thinking in the field.

As a practicing internist, I find myself discussing issues related to bowel health several times a day with patients. Since most people find the topic to be taboo, they often only feel comfortable bringing it up with their doctors or specialists like myself when issues arise. Sometimes I literally have to pry it out of them. That is why I was delighted to see that Jesse had so cleverly blended helpful knowledge on the subject with a playful style of humor that both entertains and educates.

I feel that the book does an excellent job of covering a wide range of relevant information pertaining to bathroom health and habits. It humorously takes readers through every step of the pooping process from the first bite to the final wipe, all the while providing helpful tips for a successful experience. It is for that reason I am excited to recommend this book as a fun and informative read. In the opinion of this doctor this is a must-have book for every bathroom!

Dr. Charles Hamori, MD is an internist in San Diego.

Introduction

Back in 2016, I was watching part of Jim Jeffries' comedy special, Freedumb, where he hilariously shares about teaching his son Hank to shit. At that moment I had a copy of Thic Nhat Hanh's little Zen book titled 'How to Sit' on my coffee table. That was when I had the silly idea for a guide on how to shit.

At that point I didn't know shit about shit, so I started doing some research. Six months later I had amassed a shitload of interesting information on the subject. I learned that shitting is arguably one of our most important routines, since the health of our shits is a good indicator of our physical and mental well-being. And as we all know, a good shit can leave you feeling great, a bad shit can throw off your whole day, and not shitting at all can leave you feeling like you're full of shit.

I hope that by the end of this book you will have a new appreciation for this under-appreciated subject. So whether you are curled up on the sofa or pinching a loaf on the can, settle in as we explore the vastly interesting topic of shit.

Chapter 1

How to Shit

Shitting is one of those necessities you learned early on in life and have probably never really bothered to think about since. Unlike other areas of your health, such as oral hygiene, where your dentist instructed you on how to better scrub or floss your pearly whites, no one has likely ever observed you during a shit and offered any suggestions for improvement. That is not to say that you have been doing it wrong, but as I have found during my research, there are plenty of ways to make shitting more pleasant and effective—even if you already take world-class shits.

Pre-Poop Checklist

Before we get into the nitty-gritty of how to make your shits less shitty, let's take a moment to discuss the importance of the Pre-Poop Checklist. Just as any responsible pilot always performs a pre-flight checklist to avoid catastrophic errors, the same advice applies to taking a shit. Pausing for a brief moment to review

Have a Great Shit

this short list can save you from possible hassle or humiliation. As is true with any important safety campaign, I have distilled it down to three simple action items: Look, Lock & Run.

Look

The first essential step is to check and make sure that the toilet paper dispenser has an ample supply to meet your wiping needs. There is nothing worse than finishing your business—only to find that you now have to go on a tactical mission with your pants down to find something to wipe your butt with.

Lock

The next step is to lock the bathroom door. This will prevent any unwanted intrusions from spouses, kids, friends, roommates, pets, or strangers during your moment of Zen.

Run

The final step is to run the fan (or open the window) if the facility has one. This does two important things. First, it cuts down on the odors of your creation, second is that the fan usually serves to hopefully drown out any offensive sounds that may happen to accompany your performance.

Chapter 1: How to Shit

Nature Calls

When nature calls, and the urge to poop is upon you, you are advised to find a toilet and do your deed. Not heeding the call and holding it in could result in your wily turd deciding to retreat back into hiding—known as reverse peristalsis—for what could be a number of hours or even days, depending on its mood. If you have to shit but need a few moments to reach a facility, and are fearful of a retreat, you can try a mild abdominal squeezing while partially relaxing your butthole—to keep it in the queue so to speak. But do so at your own risk as I don't want to be responsible for anyone accidentally crapping their pants. If the urge passes, let bygones be bygones and go do something else in the meantime. Try relaxing with a warm beverage and the poop fairy might be kind enough to make another house call sooner rather than later.

Holding The Call

You should always try to answer when Mother Nature is calling. Sure, there are times when a bathroom is not readily available and you have to hold it until you can locate a safe-house. But some of you may be routinely holding your turds captive for several hours or even days because of restroom phobias or the fear of being outed as someone who actually shits to your friends, loved ones, or co-workers. It might help to keep in mind that just about everyone shits and no one gives a shit if you shit except you.

There are some good reasons why you don't want to frequently hold in your turds when they are trying to escape. The first is that forcing a retreat for a long time will cause your poop to dry out, and it will literally become a pain in the ass in the form of constipation. Another reason to shit when you have to is that over time you can end up screwing up your rectum shape and the muscles that control your ability to poop easily. So resist the urge to resist the urge and take a dump when you have to go.

The Big Act

After heeding the call and reporting for doodie duty, you are now ready to get started on what will hopefully turn out to be a lavatory success story. The

Chapter 1: How to Shit

following sections offer some strategies to increase the odds of having a pleasant experience on the can.

Poositions

How you sit during your shit can affect how easily, and thoroughly, you complete your mission. When you sit at a right-angle, with your back straight and your feet on the ground, your internal puborectalis muscle ends up pinching your rectum, which blocks the flow of your poops. This causes you to strain more, and you end up emptying less of your load. By slightly adjusting your position you may find it easier to go like a pro.

Squat

Squatting is considered to be one of the most ergonomic positions for both sitting and shitting. People have been squatting for most of human history and it is still very common in many parts of the world. Squatting to poop, as you would imagine, involves squatting all the way down and keeping your butt off the ground—kind of like the umpire in a baseball game. Keep your knees and feet spread apart while you lean forward to better keep your balance. You then aim your butt over a hole and enjoy the most thorough poop you've ever had. Squatting is also an excellent resting position to sit in for relieving back pain.

Have a Great Shit

There are usually no good places to easily do a squat poop in a western bathroom, unless you stand on the toilet or poop in the shower—which are both dangerous and gross. But there are a couple of ways to get close to the ideal position—short of digging a hole and shitting in the yard.

Lean Over

The first and easiest position to try—especially if you are constipated—is to just lean forward as much as is comfortable while sitting on the toilet.

Chapter 1: How to Shit

You can do a mild lean by putting your hands on your knees and keeping your arms straight, or go for a more extreme lean and put your chest closer to your legs. Often this simple adjustment will make it is easier to let one go.

Poop Stools

The second position to try is to elevate your feet off the ground a few inches. There are specialized toilet stools that will help you do this. You can also grab a step stool to get a similar 5-7" elevation and see if it helps before you run out and get one. Arching your feet when you shit also raises your legs a few inches and can help achieve a more optimal position. Even if you do elevate your feet, you will still likely find it beneficial to lean forward a bit.

The Samurai

If you are game for quirky pooping variation that might just increase your flow, you can try the Samurai. In this position you keep your back straight and cross one leg over the other, so your foot is resting on your other knee, just as you might while sitting comfortably in a chair. This position supposedly gets its name from a combat scenario where you only need take one leg out of your pants when you shit so you can easily launch up to attack someone if needed.

Strain Refrain

When it comes time for launching your torpedo you should only have to apply a gentle abdominal squeezing to get things moving. If you find that you have to excessively strain or hold your breath to take a crap, you can try one of the previously mentioned ergonomic positions and see if you achieve better results. If that doesn't help, you are likely either forcing a poop before its time or you have constipation, which we cover in Chapter 3.

When you have a difficult shit and you have to hold your breath to squeeze it out—known as the Valsalva maneuver—you run the risk of injury or even death. Straining reduces blood flow into your thoracic cavity which can cause you to faint and hit your head on the way down.

Instead, try using your breathing to assist in dropping your load. Inhale with a slow deep breath and then slowly exhale, while at the same time applying a mild abdominal pressure. Continue this rhythm until you are finished. Just remember to mildly push, and don't strain, or you may be pushing up daisies before your time.

Chapter 1: How to Shit

Relax

Pooping is literally an act of letting go, and relaxing your ass is the best way to do it. You have two muscles in your anal canal called sphincters. These muscles tighten up to prevent your turds from escaping prematurely. You have an internal sphincter that works involuntarily and an external sphincter that you can control, like when you decide to hold in a shit. When you are on the pot you will want your external sphincter to be fully relaxed for an easy exit. Before you sit for a shit, take a moment to clear your mind, calm your breathing and focus on relaxing your body, especially your butthole. In other words, make shitting your moment of Zen.

Frequency

When it comes to normal pooping intervals, they can range anywhere from 3 times a day to 3 times a week depending on the person. It just depends on what feels right for you. But it is generally ideal to be going at least twice a week, otherwise you're likely to be considered to be 'full of shit'.

Depending on your lifestyle, your diet, and the cooperation of your large intestine, you may be able to develop a consistent pooping schedule that works well for you. If you work outside the home it can be nice to get your logs to roll out before you roll out of the driveway to go to work. After breakfast is a good time to aim for a consistent shit since you have had the night to digest your food. Eating a healthy breakfast stretches your stomach and often triggers the gatrocoloic reflex, which gets things moving in the right direction to make room for more food.

If you are the type of person who hits the snooze button 20 times and then runs out the door with food in your mouth, you are probably missing a nice pooping opportunity. When aiming for a morning drop it helps if you set aside some relax-time to allow for the poop fairy to make a visit. Try waking up 20 minutes before the morning buzz and then eat a relaxing breakfast with a warm beverage. Coaxing a turd in the morning is a great way to start your day and will help you feel better equipped for all the crap you have to deal with when you get to work.

Potty Time

Even though sitting on the throne may make you feel like a king, it is best to only visit the crapper when you actually have the urge to crap. Don't play the waiting game or you will be more likely to strain and force a shit. One study found that people who loiter and read on the pot were more likely to develop hemorrhoids.

Chapter 1: How to Shit

In other words don't sit and read this whole book in one sitting unless you are a speed-reader.

When you do sit for shit, your total time on the pot should be under 10-15 minutes. If it takes much longer than that, it is probably time to switch up your diet and lifestyle.

Clean Up Time

Hopefully the tips above have assisted you in achieving a pleasant shit. But you still have a little more work to do before you can saddle up and get back on the range—unless you like cruising through the day with a crusty crack.

<u>Have a Great Shit</u>

Toilet Paper

Toilet paper, aka TP, is the standard poo remover found in most bathrooms in the US. TP is convenient in that it keeps your hands from making contact with your dirty butt, and does a decent job with cleanup. Also, yanking on a fresh roll provides abundant entertainment for toddlers and cats.

When it comes to wiping, you want to strike the right balance with the amount of toilet paper used, and the optimal technique. If you wad up too much TP, or are not thorough enough, it can be hard for the bundle to contour your crack and you will end up with skid marks in your undies. If you use too little, you risk sheet failure, and a case of poopy-hand.

When you do wipe, you might find it helpful to lean to one side and lift up slightly on one cheek to better access and wipe your butt crack. Make a few firm, but gentle passes—with new TP each time—and you should end up getting the job done. There is no correct amount of TP to use, but the more wipes you do; the more likely you are to chafe your ass—since you are essentially rubbing dry paper on your tender butthole. And speaking of wiping, it is also especially important for girls to always wipe towards the back to keep the poop away from the girly parts.

Chapter 1: How to Shit

Toilet paper is abrasive by its nature and while it's fine at removing the big stuff, it doesn't always remove the oils and smaller debris that cling to your butt after a poop. Some people may also have skin allergies to the various scents and materials that TP can contain. If toilet paper is doing the trick and leaving you feeling fresh and wonderful—then carry on. If, however it is rubbing your asshole the wrong way, or not removing all those dirty bits, then I invite you read on and take a look at some of the other ways to get your butt sparkly clean.

Wipe & Wash

Nothing—and I mean nothing—will get your hiney as shiny as using warm water and soap to clean up after a poop. If you shit at home and don't want to take a shower, you can try a 'wipe & wash' or a 'half shower'. After you are done shitting, perform a mild to moderate wiping with toilet paper, then strip naked from your waist down and hop in the bathtub. Turn on some warm water so it is going from the faucet down the drain, and then back your bum under the water. Put a small dab of soap on your fingers, then reach around and gently clean around your butthole with the soap and warm water. You will be rewarded with the cleanest ass imaginable, and will reemerge ready to take on the world with all the confidence that a clean butt can provide.

Bidets

A bidet (bih-day) is a type of fixture or device that squirts a vertical stream of water that you use to clean around your butt crack or private parts. These devices are convenient in that they remove the need for toilet paper. They are especially nice for people who cannot easily wipe their ass, or who have hemorrhoids. There are four different types of bidets that range from full bathroom fixtures to little squirt bottles.

Standard

The standard bidet is a fixture that looks like a toilet with neither tank nor seat, and is usually installed next to the toilet. These types of bidets are more commonly found in European countries. To operate, you turn on the fountain, back you bum over it, and let the water freshen up your derriere. Bidets are also nice for women who can use them when Aunt Flow comes for her monthly visit. For all the above reasons, it is not advised to use the bidet as a drinking fountain.

Chapter 1: How to Shit

Add-on

The second type of bidet attaches to a regular toilet, either between the seat and the bowl, or by replacing the entire seat assembly and lid (pictured). There are several models and versions, each with a variety of features, such as heated seats, blow drying and even musical accompaniment. Depending on the type, the spray nozzle—either manually or automatically—moves under your bum and then squirts up water.

Bum Gun

The third type of bidet is a handheld sprayer and hose that hangs next to the toilet. The sprayer, which looks like a common kitchen sink sprayer, is sometimes referred to as a 'bum gun'. As the name implies, you just grab the gun and spray your bum.

Squeeze bottle

The final type of bidet is a portable handheld squeeze bottle that has a specialized long tip with a right-angle to squirt water up your crack. While sitting on the toilet, your reach around, point the nozzle up your butt crack and squeeze the bottle. These are great to have when you want a sparkly-clean ass and don't have access to a shower or standard bidet.

Wet Wipes

While you may not see the need to lather up or straddle a fountain after a poop, you might agree that TP is a bit lacking in its ability to leave you feeling fresh and clean. You may then be delighted with the convenience and cleanliness achievable with wet wipes—also known as baby wipes or moist towelettes. Since wet wipes are the more costly wiping option—and not as environmentally friendly as TP—you can start with a few passes of toilet paper and then finish with a wet wipe or two. These wipes are fairly big and durable, so you can fold them in half after each pass to a get few extra wipes out of a single sheet.

Chapter 1: How to Shit

Because wet wipes often contain alcohol, you may find your hiney isn't so happy after using them. You can look for wipes that are unscented, or that contain other niceties such as aloe and vitamin E—to pamper your tender tush.

Clear The Air

Once you flush the toilet and dispose of any evidence, you may feel compelled to try removing any olfactory traces from the crime scene. Following are a few methods to help you accomplish your mission. As mentioned in the beginning of this chapter, running the fan or opening the window when you first enter the bathroom will usually cut down on the smell and clear the air fast. Another technique is to flush as you poop to minimize the odors—but this technique doesn't get rid of any fart vapors and obviously wastes water.

If the fan, window, or flushing isn't cutting it, you only have two options: either deal with it or try a cover up.

Air fresheners

You are probably already familiar with aerosol bathroom sprays or plug-in air fresheners. These products fill the air and either leave you feeling happy with the aromatic scent—or gagging for some fresh air. But be warned, fragrances or aerosol scents will simply end up mixing with your poop odors—which can make for its own sort of repulsive aroma. Fresh roses and fresh poop, how lovely! Less is often more when dispensing it, and choosing mild scents will generally be less offensive to others.

Toilette Sprays

Toilet sprays claim to create a barrier above the water to trap the odors after your turd takes a dip. You are instructed to spray the toilet water several times before you poop to keep the odors at bay—which sometimes works.

Alternatives

If you don't want to buy commercial sprays with unknown ingredients, you can make a simple spray. Water blended with a few drops of your favorite essential oils and rubbing alcohol, into a small spray bottle, can be used as either an air freshener or a toilet spray. Another option is to place a vanilla scented candle in the bathroom (no need to burn it). And yet another option is to keep a sachet—which is a small bag that contains ingredients—such as sandalwood, cedar or lavender, near the toilet.

Chapter 1: How to Shit

Hacks

If you are desperate for some kind of cover up and find yourself without any of the above scented accessories, you can get creative and try to make you own improvised air freshener on the spot. This can be done, with varying degrees of success by wafting a scented item such as hand lotion, shampoo or conditioner, breath spray, perfume, hairspray or even bathroom cleaner if you are really desperate.

Matches

An old standard when it comes to cover-ups has been to light a match and quickly blow it out to cover the smell. Technically, this works because the sulphur released at ignition (not the smoke or flame) masks the odor by numbing the nose a bit. If you do this, make sure there are no nearby smoke alarms, and please do not catch anything on fire.

The Bottom Line

The final option is to just deal with the fact that the bathroom often smells for a few minutes after someone takes a shit. So what if you made a stinker? Just be kind (or not) and warn any incoming shitters if the smell is really bad.

Clean Hands

If you ever worked in the food industry or were raised by someone who was doing even a half-ass job at parenting, you likely already got the memo to thoroughly wash your hands with soap and water after you take a shit. This not only keeps you healthy, it also prevents you from making other people sick. Since the bathroom has some of the highest concentration of unfriendly bacteria, you will likely come into contact with fecal matter—even if you are careful.

Washing your hands with soap and water for 15-20 seconds—about long enough to sing Happy Birthday

Chapter 1: How to Shit

twice—will remove the harmful bacteria from your hands and give you a clean bill of health. You can even sing out loud while you are doing it if you want to weird-out the other people in the bathroom. For more tips on keeping your hands free from contamination afterwards, check out the germ section in the Going Public chapter.

Have a Great Shit

Chapter 2

Poop School

There are some essential subjects that are rarely covered in school, such basics as how to stay happily married, how to manage your finances, or how to make a good shit. Luckily, I am here to complete your education as it pertains to the latter. In the following chapter, you will discover that having good shits raises your chances of living a longer, healthier, and happier life, and that is something worth giving a shit about. So hop aboard the short bus, and let's take a ride to Poop School!

Have a Great Shit

It helps to think of your body as a set of complex systems that all work together to keep you alive so you can complain about your life. Imbalances in any one system can cause problems in other areas—and many times those problems show up in the toilet. Your poops are an excellent indicator of your overall health and are worthy of your attention if they start getting out of whack.

The following list represents the most common factors and conditions that directly affect your turds. These are: water, fiber, food sensitivities, drugs, hormones, and exercise. If you are experiencing results that are less than satisfactory on the pot, you will want to check if any of these areas are in need of more attention. Let's take a closer look at each.

Water

Shit is mostly water, so if you are not drinking enough of it, your turds will be drier, harder, and more difficult to pass. Your body also requires water to more effectively send your poops down the poop chute. Aim to chug at least 6-8 glasses of water a day (roughly two quarts, two liters, or half a gallon, depending on your preferred units of measurement). Be sure to drink even more than that if you are exercising or in hot or dry weather. A good way to know if you are drinking

Chapter 2: Poop School

enough is if you are peeing at least four times a day. If your piss is either clear or light yellow in color then you get a gold star. If, however, your piss is the color of an old school bus, then it is time to start chugging some water. In case you need a reminder to drink more, set an alarm to go off every few hours, or fill a pitcher and empty it throughout the day.

Since we are on the topic of water, you might be surprised to learn that not all fluids add water to your body. Some beverages are diuretics, which actually cause you to piss out more than you drink. Alcohol (beer, wine and liquor) all dehydrate you by making you pee more than normal, which can give you constipation. For every alcoholic drink you consume, you end up losing up to 4 times as much water through your piss! Dehydration is also what makes your hangovers worse. So chug down some water between alcoholic drinks and you may stave off a bad hangover and stop a case of constipation.

Much of the world is happily dependant on caffeine to make it through the morning or day—most commonly in the form of soda, coffee or tea. Unfortunately caffeine too is a diuretic. Coffee—the world's favorite morning beverage—can have mixed results depending on the person. Even though most coffee is caffeinated and acts as a diuretic, it can also act as a mild laxative for some people, YMMV (Your Mileage May Vary). Most sodas and fizzy drinks contain high amounts sugar, salt to make you thirst for more, and of course, caffeine. This combination not only adds fat, but also invites constipation. And as if all of that isn't bad enough, high amounts of caffeine cause the body to release adrenaline and cortisol which can make you tense and stressful, adding to your pooping woes.

Happy-Poop Foods

When you eat healthy foods, you have a good chance at creating healthier shits. That is because healthy

Chapter 2: Poop School

foods are generally lower in fat and higher in dietary fiber, which is the ideal ingredient for making a nice turd. Whole, unprocessed foods and grains give you the best chance of sucking down some healthy nutrients and packing in some fiber.

So what is dietary fiber anyway? It turns out that there are two distinctly different types. **Soluble fiber**—or fiber that dissolves and absorbs water—gives a good poop it's nice smooth texture, and helps move your turd through your digestive tract. **Insoluble fiber**—which does not dissolve in water—mostly stays intact through digestion and adds roughage and bulk to your turd so that it doesn't pass too quickly. Ideally it's good to eat a mix of both fibers to help keep your poops nicely formed for a smooth and easy exit. Too much soluble fiber and your food slips through without proper nutrient absorption, too much insoluble fiber can slow down your turds.

You can experiment by consuming these two fibers in different ratios to regulate your poops and their frequency. For loose or watery poops, you want to eat more foods that are higher in insoluble fiber, or conversely eat soluble fiber foods when you are dealing with harder shits. For example, if you want a nice poop exit in the morning, go for less insoluble fiber and more soluble fiber the night before. Just

Have a Great Shit

remember to go slow when adding fiber to your diet and gradually increase your intake over a number of days or weeks—otherwise you might pay the price with a pissed-off gut and unpleasant shits.

So now that we know how fiber makes our shits happy, how much of it should we eat? According to the USDA, the recommended daily amount is **38g** for men (or 30g for men older than 50), and **25g** for women (or 21g for women older than 50).

Ok great, so how much is a gram of fiber? If you buy packaged foods, you will find it printed on the nutrition label. But the best foods for fiber—whole foods—often don't come in a box or package. Lucky for you I have compiled and ranked the fiber content from highest to lowest for many common whole foods using the USDA's nutrition database. Included here is the amount of soluble and insoluble fiber for a variety of foods, so that you can adjust your intake of each fiber type to better match your specific pooping goals.

Chapter 2: Poop School

Fiber food list

		Fruit		
Total Fiber (g)	Serving Size	Foods	Soluble Fiber	Insoluble Fiber
7.3	½ Cup	**Figs, dried**	46%	54%
6.1	½ Cup	**Prunes, dried**	58%	41%
4.75	½ Cup	**Apricots, dried**	55%	45%
4	½ Cup	**Raspberries**	27%	73%
2.75	½ Cup	**Pears**	38%	62%
2.7	½ Cup	**Raisins**	50%	50%
2.2	½ Cup	**Apple, w/skin**	35%	65%
1.8	½ Cup	**Blueberries**	21%	79%
1.5	½ Cup	**Banana**	27%	73%
1.5	½ Cup	**Orange**	62%	38%
1.5	½ Cup	**Strawberries**	39%	61%
1	½ Cup	**Grapefruit**	68%	32%
1	½ Cup	**Tomato** (yes it is a fruit)	10%	90%
0.4	½ Cup	**Grapes**	68%	32%

Have a Great Shit

Total Fiber (g)	Serving Size	Foods	Soluble Fiber	Insoluble Fiber
4.4	½ Cup	**Green Peas**	30%	70%
2.8	½ Cup	**Asparagus**	60%	40%
2.4	½ Cup	**Potato, w/skin**	30%	70%
2	½ Cup	**Green Beans**	25%	75%
1.6	½ Cup	**Corn**	12%	88%
1.3	½ Cup	**Kale**	28%	72%
1.3	½ Cup	**Broccoli**	50%	50%
1.1	½ Cup	**Carrots**	55%	45%
1	½ Cup	**Brussel Sprouts**	52%	48%
.9	½ Cup	**Zucchini**	52%	48%
.7	½ Cup	**Cauliflower**	40%	60%
.8	½ Cup	**Celery (raw)**	41%	59%
.5	½ Cup	**Lettuce (raw)**	20%	80%

Chapter 2: Poop School

Cooked Beans				
Total Fiber (g)	Serving Size	Foods	Soluble Fiber	Insoluble Fiber
7.8	½ Cup	**Lentils**	42%	58%
7.7	½ Cup	**Pinto beans**	74%	26%
7.5	½ Cup	**Black beans**	55%	45%
5.6	½ Cup	**Kidney beans**	50%	50%
5.5	½ Cup	**Blackeyed peas**	53%	47%

Cooked Rice, Pasta & Grains				
Total Fiber (g)	Serving Size	Foods	Soluble Fiber	Insoluble Fiber
3	½ Cup	**Barley**	78 %	22%
2.6	½ Cup	**Quinoa**	40%	60%
2.3	½ Cup	**Whole grain pasta**	25%	75%
1.6	½ Cup	**Brown rice**	92%	8%
.9	½ Cup	**White pasta**	44%	66%
.3	½ Cup	**White rice**	20%	80%

Have a Great Shit

		Nuts and Seeds		
Total Fiber (g)	Serving Size	Foods	Soluble Fiber	Insoluble Fiber
5	Tbsp	**Psyllium seed husks**	88%	22%
2.8	Tbsp	**Flaxseeds**	56%	44 %
1.1	Tbsp	**Sesame seeds**	21%	79%
7.5	½ Cup	**Almonds**	16%	84%
7.3	½ Cup	**Pistachio** nuts	24%	76%
7.1	½ Cup	**Sunflower seeds**	36%	64%
6.2	½ Cup	**Peanuts**	47%	53%
5.2	½ Cup	**Pecans**	20%	80%
4.2	½ Cup	**Walnuts**	19%	81%
2	½ Cup	**Cashews**	10%	90%
3.6	3 Cups	**Popcorn popped**	1%	99%

Chapter 2: Poop School

Sad-Poop Foods

Some foods taste great on the way in, but they can be a literal pain in the ass on the way out. Processed foods, and fatty meats and cheeses are often high in fat and sugar, and low in fiber—which increases the risk of a traffic jam in your ass. It is almost always ok to eat these foods in moderation, as long as you are also eating plenty of healthy stuff, like the goodies listed in the fiber chart. Sure, it might require some discipline and added expense, but knowing how much nicer your shits and your health will be could be just the motivation you need. Here are some common foods that can give you bad shits when consumed in excess.

Fried foods

Fried foods like donuts, breaded meats and French fries are (you guessed it!) high in fat. If you haven't already heard, these foods are pretty bad for your heart and arteries and can also give you shittier shits. Less is more with these guys.

Cheese & dairy

Cheese is essentially fat—which is why it tastes so damned good! As a rule of thumb, look at the package and try limiting yourself to two servings per meal. You might also find that dairy gives you constipation—or the shits—depending on your tolerance to lactose (milk sugar from dairy).

Fatty Red Meat

When you eat fatty red meat, you may notice that your shits take longer to work through the pipes, and they are stinkier as well. This is because red meats are high in fat and iron and low in fiber. This can be helped by eating smaller portions, thoroughly chewing each piece, and choosing low-fat cuts of meat.

Food Allergies & Sensitivities

Food allergies and sensitivities can affect people in all sorts of shitty ways—anything from bad gas to

Chapter 2: Poop School

anaphylactic shock and death! The difference between the two is that sensitivities are more mild and common, whereas allergies are more severe and sometimes lethal. It can also be tricky to pinpoint these 'enemy foods', because after eating them, symptoms may not appear for up to 48 hours.

The usual suspects are: peanuts, tree nuts, fish, shellfish, milk (dairy), eggs, soy and wheat (gluten). If after eating these foods you experience bloating, diarrhea, gas, etc., you may want to test if these foods don't like you. The way to do that is to keep track of what you eat and when you eat it, then take note of any symptoms in a personal health journal, or by using a food allergy app. You can also try an elimination diet and avoid eating the suspected foods for a few weeks and see if symptoms disappear. Then gradually start eating them again, and notice if symptoms reappear. If you think you have more serious allergies, you can see a professional allergist and they can administer specific tests.

Once you narrow in and eliminate your enemy foods, you can steer clear of them at home, or when ordering at restaurants. Yeah, it sucks to be that person with a list of dietary no-no's, but it's better to speak up, than pay the price on the pot.

Drugs

Americans have increasingly become a nation of drug users—not to mention the illegal substances. People are popping more prescription pills than ever before. While these medications may provide relief from the targeted ailment, they can also take their toll on the tummy. Drug companies often warn that their meds may mess up your insides with anything from constipation to vomiting, or even death. It is also not uncommon to have to use combinations of drugs to counteract the negative effects of the other drugs.

If you trace your poo problems back to pill popping, you may want to consult your doctor about alternatives. Also, making healthy adjustments to the areas outlined in this chapter may do wonders for your overall health—possibly reducing or eliminating the ailments you are currently medicating.

Chapter 2: Poop School

Mood

Negative mental emotions, such as stress, anxiety & depression can all adversely affect your bowels, and can cause anything from constipation, diarrhea, or persistent conditions like IBS. That is because your brain and your gut are in constant communication with each other by way of an internal telephone network, called the vagus nerve. When your brain is feeling emotions like stress or depression, your gut flow is disrupted and produces bad shits. Everyone has occasional ups and downs, but long-term negative emotions are hard on your health and your turds.

The gut-brain connection also works the other way, so when your gut is having problems, it can cause bad moods. If you eat 'pleasure foods' that are high in fat or sugar, they give a quick energy boost, followed by a low-energy crash that can leave you feeling irritable. And when you are in a bad mood, it's tempting to seek comfort foods that are often high in fat and sugar—which creates a viscous cycle. When you are feeling grumpy or angry for no good reason, take a moment to think back to what you last ate and see if that could be the possible reason behind your pissy attitude.

Exercise

So far we have been finding that what is good for your body is generally good for your poops, and exercise is no exception. Regular aerobic activity benefits your bowels by increasing circulation and strengthening your muscles—which can help you heave out nice turds.

While a good cardio workout, such as running or cycling, will really get your blood flowing, other low impact activities like yoga, swimming, or even going for a 20 minute walk, will also give added benefits. Exercise has also been shown to improve your mood, which we now know is also good for your turds.

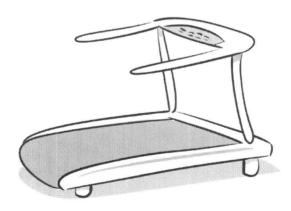

Chapter 2: Poop School

So dust off that workout equipment, get off your ass, and move every day. Your gut will likely reward you with better shits and a better mood!

Making a Turd

Now that we have covered which ingredients and habits will most likely yield the best results on the pot, let's get busy making a turd! In the next section we learn how to properly send the food on its incredible journey, where it is magically transformed from food into energy, and finally into a lovely poop. We then conclude with a section on how to grade the end results once your poop crosses the finish line.

Chew on This

After you prepare your shit-friendly meal or snack, it is time to get it down your gullet. The best way to do that is to cut, or bite it into small morsels, and get to work chewing on it. Chewing your food breaks it down into smaller pieces so it can be better digested and more quickly turned into the energy you need to keep reading this book.

Thorough chewing allows for a more even coating of your food with the enzymes in your saliva, which helps with digestion. It also produces softer material that is easier on your intestines. Well-chewed food minimizes the amount of bacteria and fungi that make it into your intestines, which reduces indigestion and bad farts. Thorough chewing also lengthens your eating time, and may reduce the amount of food you need to eat to feel full. That's because the stomach takes about 20 minutes to tell the brain that the tank is full. Slowing down prevents you from over-eating, and gives your brain some time to get the message.

Finally, you will probably want to wash some of that food down with some water. Wait to drink until after you have fully swallowed, so your digestive enzymes will not be diluted, then gulp away.

Gut Reaction

Before we get into the fascinating journey that your recently chewed food is about to go on, let's take a moment to understand the role and importance of the gastrointestinal tract (GI), or gut. Aside from your brain, your gut has the second largest concentration of neurons in your body, and as mentioned, the brain and gut are in constant communication. Have you ever noticed that your stomach starts doing the thinking when you start getting hungry? This also means that if you are in a panicked situation, your brain can give your intestines the orders that will literally make you

Chapter 2: Poop School

lose your shit. Research shows that your gut is responsible for producing up to 90% of your body's serotonin (the naturally occurring good-mood happy drug). So keep your tummy happy and it will do the same for you.

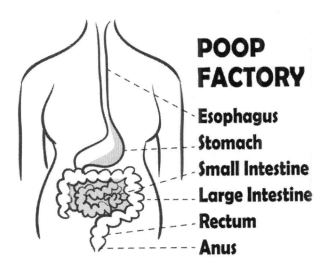

Ok, so now back to the thrilling digestive process. After your chewed-up food slides down the hatch, it enters the muscular tube called the esophagus. This tube uses contractions to move the food down towards the stomach, which takes just a few seconds. When it reaches the stomach, powerful muscle walls mix and grind the food by adding enzymes to break it

Have a Great Shit

down over the course of 4-5 hours. Once finished, the food paste then travels along a twenty-foot coiled tube called the small intestine. Over the next 5-7 hours the numerous bacteria in your gut—roughly 100 trillion—aid in the digestion and absorption into the bloodstream.

Once complete, the remaining waste moves on to the 5-foot tube called the colon—or large intestine. This final step takes about 24-40 hours, where it dries out and is prepped for launch. Once drying is complete, the upper sphincter muscle automatically releases your turd into the rectal canal. This is when you get the urge to find a toilet. Once there, you give the final launch codes to release the outer sphincter and drop your bomb.

The whole digestion process takes anywhere from 24-72 hours. During that time, your body—with the aid of its trillions of friends—has turned your wonderful meal into caloric energy, and finally, a turd. That also means that your most recent shit was the likely by-product of foods that you ate a few meals prior. Even now, as you are reading this book, your gut is hard at work carefully crafting your next log.

After you shit, and before flushing your masterpiece, take a peek to make sure that everything looks normal. As mentioned before, your turds can tell you a

Chapter 2: Poop School

lot about your physical and mental health, like how well you are eating, if you are stressing too much, or if you've got bigger problems that need tending to. So let's move on and grade your work.

Poop Grades

Following are a list of common poop-types to help you identify and grade your poops. While this grading system is purely for fun—and not a complete indicator of your health or self-worth—you may find it helpful in your quest to achieving nice turds. The first thing to notice when gazing upon your newly minted poop, is its shape anc texture. You can then use this grading system to see how you did.

Smooth Move

Way to go! This is the gold standard of poops. These should have a nice form, be relatively soft and smooth, approximately six to eight inches in length, and best of all, be easy to pass. Your parents will be so proud!

Soft Nuggets

You might want to literally get your shit together and add some more fiber to your diet. Fiber—as we discovered earlier—is the magic ingredient that gives a healthy turd its longer, lovelier form.

Pencils

Pencil-thin turds are usually due to stress, or internal problems. If you are not stressed, but are still dispensing thin turds, your gut is probably not too

Chapter 2: Poop School

happy and needs to get looked at. If stress is causing your skinny turds, then deal with that shit! Life is too short to worry or stress out about stupid stuff.

Hard Rocks

You have constipation my friend. You are not alone though, millions of people suffer from it every day. The bad news is that you have to get those painful lumps out of your ass, and they may scrape up your rectum and cause bleeding. The good news is that constipation can often be easily cured by adding fiber, exercise, and hydration. See Chapter 3 for constipation remedies.

Have a Great Shit

Hard Log

This is what really bad constipation looks and feels like—and you don't want it. This is the result of poops that are taking way too long to come out—like a week or more. Make some changes in your diet and exercise and get your gut back to health, or else your butthole will be paying the price.

Liquid or muddy

This is the shittiest shit! Liquid poops can have several causes, ranging from bacterial infection, to stress, to

Chapter 2: Poop School

disease. Worst of all, they sometimes make their exit unannounced. This poop receives the lowest letter grade, because not only is it an awful experience before, and during your trip to the bathroom, diarrhea kills hundreds of thousands of people every year—especially in developing countries.

Poop Colors

While most healthy and happy poops will be some shade of brown, it is not unusual to have a different colored poop from time to time, depending on what you have been eating. If however, your shits begin to change color for more than a few days, you will want to determine the cause.

Brown

Brown gets the gold when it comes to poop color. Even better is if it is a dark shade of brown—like a chocolate bar. This means that your bile ducts and pancreas are working nicely—which is good if you want to stay alive.

Green

Green shit is often the result of eating lots of leafy-green veggies, so no need to worry if that is the case. Other factors can include medications, or too much stress, which can cause your shit to move to quickly through the pipes and skipping proper nutrient absorption.

Yellow

There can often be a number of factors that produce yellow shits, none of which should cause too much concern unless they persist over time. Yellow shits may be a sign that there is a lot of fat present that is not being properly digested. Similar to green shit, yellow shit can also be the result of stress, or anxiety that is moving your shit through your system too fast. Many gastrointestinal diseases or liver disorders also produce yellow turds, so that is something to be aware of if yellow shits persist.

Gray

Pale or clay-colored poops are usually not a very good sign over time, and can indicate pancreas or liver problems. Grays are the result of not enough bile (the brown stuff) from the pancreas. This lightening in the color of your poops can occur gradually, so be on the lookout.

Red

Red poops can have a few different causes. If you eat a lot of beets or consume foods and drinks with red dye, this will affect your poop color. It can also be a sign of

Chapter 2: Poop School

bleeding in the stomach, or intestines. If you can't figure out the cause, definitely get it checked out.

Black

If your poop is black, smelly, and tarry, it may be bad news and time get it looked at quickly. This is possibly the presence of blood in your upper GI tract that can be dangerous or deadly. Iron supplements may also cause this condition.

Blue

A rare phenomena! You are either a Smurf, or you are eating blue colored foods like blueberries. No need to worry so long as your poops don't have a case of the blues for too long.

Poop Size

A typical turd is roughly 6-8 inches in length, and 1-1/2 inches in diameter. These sizes are just a guideline, and yours may be bigger or smaller. If they are too small, like rabbit pellets, you likely are not eating enough fiber, and have constipation. On the other hand, if you are honking out giant anacondas, you may need to be pooping a little more frequently.

Buoyancy

Most turds will sink like the Titanic. However, it is not necessarily a problem if they float. Floaters are usually the result unprocessed fats, or air, or gas trapped in your turd, from digestion and breathing. When you swallow air, or carbonation, it ends up coming out of one end or the other, either in the form of a burp, a fart, or being trapped in a floating poop. If everything else looks and smells normal, floaters are nothing to worry about. If, however, your poops float entirely above the water, then you have a case of the 'holy shits'.

Smell

Poop usually smells bad. That is Mother Nature's way of telling us "don't eat that". But there are times when your poop might smell REALLY bad, and you will know the difference. If this is the case for any length of time—especially with a change in color—it may be time to see your doc.

Taste

Gross! Don't ever taste your turds!

Chapter 2: Poop School

Final Thoughts

While I have done my best to give you an overview of shitting, this is by no means a complete resource. If you still have questions or concerns, ask your doctor or jump on the interwebs and do some searching on your own. Chances are that you are not alone with your questions—or misery—and you will find possible answers or maybe even a community to share your woes with. If you do search the web, don't get yourself into a frenzied panic if your symptoms are similar to other life-threatening worst-case scenarios. As you have learned, there are a lot of factors that can give you bad or weird shits, so just get it checked out if your problems persist.

You may also find it helpful to log your unusual logs in a log book, along with what you have been recently eating or doing. This can help you trace any poo problems back to the offending food or condition, and can also serve as a timeline for you and your doctor if problems persist. Logging in a paper journal can also come in handy for those times when you run out of TP and need to tear out a page to wipe your ass.

Have a Great Shit

Chapter 3

Pain in the Ass

In the previous chapter we covered how factors such as diet, exercise, hydration, and medication, can all affect the quality and ease of your poops. And while making the effort to have better shits will likely pay off, there will still be times when you fall off the wagon, and wind up with a case of constipation, or worse, be caught off guard with a sneak attack of diarrhea. During these low-points, we all become desperate for some immediate relief on the can. Below are just a few of the more common poop-related annoyances, and a few tips on how to cope.

Constipation

Constipation is quite simply the result of not pooping frequently enough, which causes your turds to dry out, and become hard. Hard shits are a pooping ailment that affects millions of Americans each year. They are usually the result of getting out of balance in any of the areas we covered in Poop School. Women are also more likely than men to experience constipation. The internal female anatomy—as you probably already know—has a few extra parts built in. The reproductive organs can and do move around during menstruation, putting added pressure on the rectum, which often results in constipation or symptoms of IBS.

Immediate Relief

If you are on the can and struggling with a difficult shit, there are a few remedies you can try to help ease your suffering. The very first thing is make sure that you are not dehydrated. Drink some water if you are. Next, when you are on the toilet, lean forward or use a poop stool to elevate your feet. Try to relax your body with easy deep breathing. If that does not help, begin to gently massage your lower abdomen. And if you are really desperate, you can try a perineum massage while seated on the toilet. This is a gentle massaging of the area between your genitals and butt hole (also known as the "t'ain't," because it ain't the gentials and it ain't the ass)—and can sometimes stimulate your system into action.

Laxatives

If massages and different positions are not helping, you are probably in need of a laxative. Natural laxatives are a good choice because they don't contain the harsh chemicals often found in manufactured varieties. A very effective natural option is eating a few prunes, or drinking a glass of warm prune juice,

Chapter 3: Pain in the Ass

which often provides relief by clearing the bowels. Other remedies include taking a tablespoon of psyllium husk, or a magnesium supplement. Rye bread is also said to have a laxative effect.

Over-the-counter laxatives can do the job if used in moderation. Keep in mind that that the quicker a laxative works, the easier it is to overcorrect the problem, and end up with painful bloating and watery shits. Also, taking commercial laxatives for longer than 1-2 weeks can lead to digestive dependency, which makes it difficult to shit without them, causing even more serious constipation. So don't overdo it, or you may have to check your gut into rehab.

Prevention

It may seem obvious, but you want to avoid foods that make you constipated—when you are in fact already constipated. Ease up on the high-fat foods and aim for more soluble fiber. If you are keeping a poop journal or notice that you haven't pooped for a day or two longer than normal, you should take evasive action sooner rather than later and avoid further constipation. By changing your diet, hydration, stress, or exercise routine, you should be able to get back to normal within a few days.

Diarrhea

The average person gets a case of the shits about four times a year. Most people are afflicted with acute diarrhea, which comes on quickly and goes away within a week or two. It is usually caused by a virus, or parasite, or by eating really spicy food and pissing off your gut. Chronic diarrhea lasts longer, and may be the result of IBS, or other digestive disease.

Immediate Relief

If you have acute symptoms, try an anti-diarrheal medication, as prescribed on the box, or by a pharmacist. It is best to avoid foods that are high in soluble fiber, or otherwise act as laxatives—for obvious reasons. Rehydration is also important because you have been shitting out water. Drink fluids with electrolytes, or other high-sodium liquids such as soup broth. Avoid spicy or sweet foods and stick to eating bland foods such as the BRAT diet: Bananas, Rice, Applesauce & Toast, until symptoms subside. Just be sure to stay close to a toilet for a few hours. Also beware of sharts—those sneaky shit-farts—after a recent recovery from diarrhea.

Prevention

Diarrhea is usually the result of a bacterial infection. Those nasty bacteria can get into your body from the

Chapter 3: Pain in the Ass

food you consume, but also from your contaminated hands touching your eyes, nose, or mouth. Thoroughly washing your hands, fruit and produce, or anything else that might have germs is a good start. Undercooked or spoiled food that is left unrefrigerated is also a haven for bad bacteria. Finally, water that is not properly treated—often in undeveloped countries—will give you bad shits and also make you sick, so go for bottled water in those situations.

Hemorrhoids

Hemorrhoids—or ass grapes—are enlarged veins under the skin, either inside or outside of your butthole. These are caused by excessive pressure due to straining on the pot, sitting or walking too much, being obese, being pregnant, or just having bad genes. There are two types of hemorrhoids, and both of them suck. Internal hemorrhoids are—as you would expect—on the inside of the rectum, and external ones are, (of course!) on the outside near the butthole. While hemorrhoids bleed when you poop, they are not considered dangerous, and will usually go away within a few weeks. If, however, they do not retreat in a timely manner, your doctor may recommend treatments to shrink or remove those little devils.

Relief

Hemorrhoids are a real pain the ass, causing quite a bit of discomfort. You can soak your butt in a warm bath, or a purpose-built sitz bath, a few times a day to reduce the swelling. Another option is to gently press against external hemorrhoids, which will temporarily reduce their size. Try sitting on an ice pack or pillow if you need relief while using a chair. Spread some hemorrhoid cream or petroleum jelly around your butthole to minimize the itching, and reduce abrasion when you shit. If wiping your butt is painful, use softer TP, or even facial tissue. Better yet, skip the dry paper, and wash up with water.

IBS

IBS, or Irritable Bowel Syndrome, is a shitty condition that can have many different symptoms and causes. It is defined as a prolonged digestive condition, such as loose stool, abdominal cramping, diarrhea, or constipation, and is said to affect as much as 20% of the population. Some people may find relief by adopting a healthy lifestyle and diet, but others may see little or no improvement and are just shit-out-of-luck. Even though IBS is not considered a serious condition—hence the syndrome designation—it can still be a highly annoying or even debilitating affliction.

Chapter 3: Pain in the Ass

Relief

Some people with IBS have success easing their symptoms by adopting a low FODMAP diet. FODMAPs (**F**ermentable, **O**ligo-, **D**i-, **M**ono-saccharides **A**nd **P**olyols) are foods that contain carbohydrates that may not absorb or digest easily, which can cause gas and bloating. If you suspect you are suffering from IBS, ask your doctor for a more accurate diagnosis, and inquire about possible treatments or diets.

Farty Foods

There is a big difference between passing a little gas, and clearing a room. If you are frequently performing the latter, start by taking a look at what you are putting in your mouth—unless of course you enjoy watching people gasp and run for the exits. It helps to know that air exits your butthole for one of two reasons. Either from swallowing air, which makes its way out of your butt, or from gasses produced in the digestive process—which are usually stinkier. While there are no long-term health consequences from having bad gas, strong farts can strain your relationships with friends and loved ones.

Prevention

Some foods are well known offenders when it comes to flatulence. Beans are the classic farty food. They contain oligosaccahride, a sugar that is not easily digested and ends up fermenting in the large intestine. Foods that contain sulphur or sulfites are also common fart-makers. These include wine, garlic, meat, fish, nuts, dried fruits and eggs. You are also more likely to rip some bad farts after eating vegetables that are high in sulphur, such as broccoli, cauliflower, brussel sprouts, cabbage, collards, and kale. Bad gas may also be a sign of an allergy or sensitivity to certain foods like dairy or nuts. And finally, non-foods such as medications can cause bad farts.

Relief

There are many natural anti-fart remedies, such as eating fennel, ginger, or peppermint tea. Some people find relief by taking activated charcoal supplements or a variety of commercial products aimed at fighting farts. If your farts are the result of swallowed air and don't stink as bad, try chewing with your mouth closed, don't inhale when you drink, and exhale before you swallow food. Also, keep in mind that carbonated drinks, candy suckers, and gum can all cause you to swallow air which causes farts.

Emergencies

Even though none of the following scenarios are life-threatening, they can induce a feeling of dread, cause

Chapter 3: Pain in the Ass

major inconvenience, or even worse than death—be the source of debilitating embarrassment.

No TP

If you follow the Pre-Poop Checklist you will lessen your chances of having to go hunting for TP after your shit. Regardless, you may find situations where there simply is none to be found, or you run out halfway through your mission.

DON'T PANIC!

Facial Tissue

This is the easiest and most sensible match to TP. So start there if you can find a tissue box nearby.

Have a Great Shit

Paper towels

I can speak from experience that you run the risk of a clog or overflow. If you use paper towels, tear them up into smaller squares and flush them more frequently.

Water

If you are fortunate enough to be at home, you can always elect to hop in the tub or shower and get your ass nice and clean.

Magazine or newsprint

Okay, now you're getting desperate, but here again, keep it to small pieces. Newsprint will also leave your ass dirty with ink, so wash your butt sooner than later. As a general courtesy, only wipe with advertisements or boring articles so as not to deprive future shitters of a good read.

The TP Tube

If you are really in a wiping bind, you can peel the layers off the toilet paper tube and end up with a few pieces of stiff and abrasive cardboard to grind against your butt. You can get them wet at the sink and they will be a little softer.

Chapter 3: Pain in the Ass

Cloth, towels, sponges

Use these only if you must, since they will either need to be laundered or thrown away afterwards. Oh, and don't stupidly try to flush them down the toilet.

Your handy hand

This will be a no-go for some of you, but this is how it is done in many countries where cultural norms dictate that the left hand is only used for wiping. If you go this route, just make sure to wash your hands really well afterwards. Then wash your hands a second time to get them really clean. Then wash them one more time, just to be sure. Ok now you are free to leave.

Your undies

If you are truly desperate, the very last resort is to wipe your ass with your underwear. You are on your own as far as advice as to what to do with them afterwards.

Get up and go

Depending on the situation, you can always suit up and waddle over to another stall or bathroom. Just keep those butt cheeks clenched!

Have a Great Shit

Clogs

There are few experiences more utterly terrifying than flushing the toilet, only to have the water level begin to rise and elevate your turd towards the edge of the bowl. Stay calm, and wait until the water stops running. Generally it won't overflow on the first flush, and sometimes the toilet will clear after sitting for a minute. You can also take this opportunity to grade the quality of your turd.

If the water level remains stubbornly high, look around for a plunger. Place the rubber end in the bowl and let the cup fill with water. Then place the cup against the toilet drain and hold the handle in a vertical position. Push straight down and up several times while keeping the cup firmly against the drain. Hopefully the water level will begin to recede and your heartbeat will return to a normal pace.

If, however, the water still does not go down after the first flush, you can risk a second flush—but you might be pushing your luck and have to deal with a turd breach. If you want to safely perform a second flush on a toilet with a tank, you can remove the tank lid and then flush again. If the water gets close to overflowing you can reach in and push the black stopper down so the bowl stops filling. Don't worry, the water in the tank has not been in the toilet bowl.

Chapter 3: Pain in the Ass

If you don't have a plunger handy, you can try using the toilet brush the same way you would with a plunger, to try and exert more water pressure down the drain. You will obliviously want to clean the brush or plunger with fresh water before your return it to its home. If you are still stuck, try adding hot water and soap to the bowl and let it sit to see if that helps loosen the clog. Chemical clog removers sometimes work, but they take time and they are often toxic—which is bad for your skin and the environment.

Hopefully one of the above methods saved the day. If not, it's time to roll up your sleeves, reach in the bowl and...I am totally kidding! Call a professional plumber or use a pro device—like a plumbing snake—to clear the clog. If you happen to clog a toilet in public or at someone's house or party, discretely ask for assistance, or for a plunger. Try not be too embarrassed, just remember, we have all been there.

Poopy Pants

Sometimes shit literally happens unannounced, and when it does it sucks being you. But hey, these events sometimes make for the funniest stories later! Maybe it's because you tried holding your poop too long. Or that spicy dish decided to make a run for the border before you could run to the toilet. Or maybe a shart

Have a Great Shit

caught you off guard. Just clench those butt cheeks hard the moment you suspect a premature exit.

Remember to stay calm and know that you will survive this. The less dramatic you are, the easier it will be to get through it. In fact, a sense of humor will go a long way right about now. The good news is that you may have gotten lucky and not shit your pants—even if it feels like it. To be sure, find a restroom and ass-ess the situation. Don't reach in your pants in public to find out. How you get to the bathroom unnoticed will depend on your level of stealth or creative distraction, just don't pull the fire alarm as a means of diverting attention.

If there is in fact a doodie in your drawers, you can elect to throw them away, clean them in the sink, or toss them in a bag to launder later. Hopefully you have a set of emergency undies nearby, otherwise you are going commando—and won't have a safety net if it happens again. Good luck!

Chapter 4

Going Public

I think it is safe to say that most of us would rather poop at home, or at least in private, given the choice. Home-shits are generally preferred because you know exactly where everything is, and there are usually no surprises or distractions, so you can better relax. There are, however, times when you will need to feed the toilet out in the real world, or on a long car trip, or camping outdoors. With a little planning and strategy, you can make the experience a little less shitty.

Shit Kit

The first bit of advice, depending on your needs, is to assemble a Shit Kit. There are a variety of goodies you can stash in your kit to make going public more bearable. Let's go through some of the more common niceties you may elect to have on-hand.

Have a Great Shit

The bag

If you don't already carry around a suitable-sized purse, start out by acquiring a small zippered hand bag for your stash that is discrete and easy to carry. Finding one with a small loop to hang on the bathroom door will allow you to keep your hands free when you are navigating the toilet. A hip-pack is also a convenient option if you don't mind looking like a dork.

Wet wipes

The most popular accessory on our list is a pack of wet wipes, aka baby wipes. These are the Swiss army knife of any shit kit. You can use them to wipe off the door handles, prep the toilet seat, and most importantly, cleanse your butthole; hopefully not all with the same wipe.

Chapter 4: Going Public

Portable Bidet

As mentioned in the first chapter, a portable bidet is a nice accessory if you want to incorporate water into your cleaning routine outside the home. The little squirt bottle types take up a little more space in your kit, but are far superior at leaving you with a shiny hiney.

Toilet Paper

Oftentimes the TP found in public potties sucks. But hey, what can you expect for free right? If you are a 2-ply snob and don't fancy wiping your ass with wafer-thin sheets, why not bring some of your own TP from home? Just remember to replenish your stock, or the next time you need it, you will be wiping like a commoner.

Medication

It is always wise to have some anti-diarrheal pills handy. Not only will it be a life-saver if you get a case of the shits but you can be a hero and come to the rescue of a distressed friend or co-worker in need.

Gloves

If you are a germophobe, or find yourself having to navigate a lavatorial crime scene, gloves can be a real treat. Once you have donned a pair, you will be free to touch all sorts of filthy and repulsive things without the need to vigorously wash your hands afterwards.

Air Freshener

You may be inclined to pack along your own air freshener, either as a courtesy to others after you poop, or to keep yourself from gagging from the noxious vapors left by the last patron. Just keep in mind that what may smell like a bundle of fresh roses to you may smell like a noxious cloud to others, so go easy with that stuff.

Clean Undies

You probably don't need to carry around an extra pair of clean underwear unless you regularly crap your pants. However, having a spare pair of clean butt-huggers stashed in your car or desk at work may come in handy some day. If, for instance, you find yourself mortified after realizing your friendly little fart was actually a shart, you will be glad you planned ahead. You can also buy lightweight disposable undies for just that purpose.

Hand sanitizer

A little bottle of hand sanitizer can come in handy if the automatic soap squirter either doesn't like you, or is out of order. Incidentally—because it contains

Chapter 4: Going Public

alcohol—it makes a great fire starter it you are having trouble getting you campfire lit.

Stall Hunting

Whether you are seeking privacy, cleanliness, or both, there are some tips that might help you achieve success in your hunt for the perfect potty. While there is no golden rule when it comes to finding a decently clean stall in the bathroom, sometimes the closest or furthest stalls from the entrance get the least use and may prove to be a bit cleaner than the rest.

Unfortunately the luxury of private pooping is not always easy to attain in a public setting. The simplest thing to do is get over it, use the closest bathroom when you have to shit—regardless if there are others nearby—and get on with your day. But if you are easily distracted by the presence, smells, or noises of fellow poopers, you may elect to go on a hunt for a quiet commode. If you are a stall-hunter, you probably already have a closely guarded list of such places where you work or frequent, but here are some tips for finding a few more.

It helps to keep an eye out for clean and convenient bathrooms before you actually have to poop. If you are potty hunting at a store, hotel, or restaurant, generally the nicer the establishment, the nicer and more private the bathrooms are. If you work in an office building, you can scope out different floors, or find an area where there are more people of the opposite sex. If you can adjust your poop schedule, you may be able to avoid more crowded times of the day, like mornings, or after lunch, when the potties are more likely to be crowded with poopers. You might discover where the VIPs do their business—provided that the bathroom entrance doesn't have an armed guard or a retinal scanner.

Germs

Aside from a lack of privacy, germs are probably the biggest fear when using a public potty. While it is true that just about every surface in a public bathroom has the potential to disperse bacteria, it doesn't mean that you need to avoid public potties like the plague. A good defense will keep those pesky germs at bay and allow you to take a worry-free shit when you have to go.

Chapter 4: Going Public

Interestingly, fecal matter (aka shit) is not dangerous. However, the minute it sees the light of day, it attracts dangerous bacteria, like E.coli and staph, which cause serious illnesses. These bad bacteria enter our bodies through our eyes, nose or mouth, so when you forget to wash your hands, you are exposing yourself and others to the risk of diarrhea, hepatitis, or food poisoning. Assume that your unwashed hands are in fact the potential danger, thoroughly clean them after using the toilet, and try not to re-contaminate them after they are clean.

Public doors are perfect places for viruses and bacteria to transfer from one person to the next, and that goes double for restroom exits. Assume that the door and handle have been contaminated by dozens of potty hands. Do not touch them with your bare hands if you can help it. Often you can lean against the restroom door on the way in, but need to pull the handle on the way out. If you do, make sure those fingers are clean before eating or touching your eyes or nose. You can snag an extra paper towel from the sink and use it as a hand-condom, or use your ring and pinky finger to pull it open, which keeps your main fingers clean for picking your nose later.

The lowly floor in a bathroom stall likely has the largest concentration of bacteria in a public bathroom. It is best to keep your belongings either on your person or hanging from a hook. Even better, don't bring in extra stuff at all if you can help it. Apart from your Shit Kit, leave your belongings with a friend or a store clerk if you are out shopping. This will help you more easily navigate the stall, prevent contamination, and reduce the likelihood of leaving your unintended shit behind.

Seat Prep

Contrary to popular belief, the toilet seat can be one of the least germy areas in a public bathroom—so you can stop freaking out about sitting on it. Give it a wipe with some TP or disinfectant if you wish, and plop your

Chapter 4: Going Public

ass down without worry. You won't catch anything by sitting on it.

If you are still skittish about making contact or encounter a wet toilet seat, you can wipe down the surface first, then lay down a length of TP on each side, or use one of those giant paper bum barriers. If a paper barrier for your derriere is not an acceptable option, some people— especially women—opt for a hover. This is why you practice the chair pose in yoga right? It might help to find a stall with a handrail in case you lose your balance. Also, if you want to avoid splash-back from the potty, lay a few pieces of TP on the water before you poop. People who hover often make a bigger mess than sitters, so don't be a shit - clean up any mishaps or splashes.

Auto Fl*&!sh toilets

These one-eyed menaces are designed to hassle you by flushing before you're done, or by holding you hostage and not flushing when you want to leave. You can try to blind the beast by putting a paper towel over the sensor so you can poop in peace. If the toilet is being rebellious and won't flush after you are done, use the small button on the top, or near the sensor.

Passing the baton

At some public potties you will have to flag down the gatekeeper in charge of the coveted bathroom key and convince them that you are worthy to shit in their toilet. If you pass the test, you will likely be handed an obscenely large object such as a bowling pin or car tire with a key attached to it so you don't steal it.

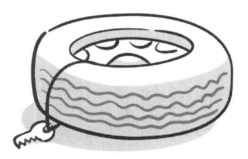

This baton should be treated as if it were radioactive, considering the excess of bacteria it likely possesses after being passed from one person to the next. Once you get inside the bathroom and stow the baton, wash your hands before touching anything else. After you use the potty and are done washing up, you can use a paper towel to handle it on the way out.

Chapter 4: Going Public

Outdoor shits

Shitting in the woods is the most primitive way to let one go, since you will be forgoing all the niceties that modernity has bestowed upon us. That said, you can use the experience to connect with how your ancestors shat for most of human history. Also, as we covered earlier, squatting is a natural and ergonomic position for your body—so take a moment to enjoy it.

You will want to pick a private spot, out of view, and at least a few dozen yards from where people travel or where your campmates are enjoying their breakfast. Take along a spade shovel, your Shit Kit and a good attitude. Some wilderness areas do not allow you to leave your TP or wipes behind, so take along a baggie for your paper waste if needed.

As you wander off in search of pooping paradise, you are advised to look for a spot next to a tree or a rock for privacy—and also to use for balance, in case you lose your balance and start to fall over during your poop. Be careful not to let your hands or butt cheeks come into contact with irritant plants such as poison oak, ivy or sumac, or you might end up furiously scratching your ass for the next week. Also beware if there are mosquitoes or black flies buzzing around, because those suckers will surely want a piece of your ass. If that is the case, you may want to put some

Have a Great Shit

skeeter repellant on your butt cheeks, and wash it off when you are done.

Once you have claimed your spot and are out of visual range, dig a hole about 6 inches wide and 6 inches deep. Then assume the lovely squat with your bum over the target and drop your load. If you happen to find yourself stuck in the woods without any TP, you can use a smooth stone or leaves. It is best to avoid wiping with pinecones or small furry animals, unless you are very careful.

Be sure to give your turd a proper burial using the dirt you dug out. Finally, put a few rocks over the mound to make it more difficult for critters or your campmates to excavate your buried treasure. And that is it—mission accomplished! Now you can get back to enjoying the great outdoors knowing that you made a valuable contribution to the beautiful landscape.

Chapter 4: Going Public

Pits & Portos

On the convenience scale, pit toilets and portable potties fall somewhere in between shitting in the woods, and using a regular bathroom. On the plus side, they usually offer privacy, a seat, and on occasion, a roll of wafer-thin toilet paper. The biggest drawback, however, is that they often stink to high heaven. If the odors are particularly acrid, you can try breathing through your mouth, breathing through a scarf, or wearing a military-grade gas mask. Often these rustic outhouses are without electricity, so a headlamp is advised, especially at night. When you are finished in a pit toilet, remember to put the lid back down to cut down on the smell and flies, and then dash back outside so that you don't pass out from a lack of oxygen.

Vacation Constipation

One of the most common and annoying side-effects of travelling and vacations is that your poops will sometimes go into hiding. This can be a real drag and prevent you from fully enjoying your trip. The main causes are messed up pooping schedules, eating different or bad foods, and elevated stress levels. Following are some ideas to keep your poops from taking a vacation when you do.

Travelling Turds

The trick to making your travels more pleasant is to try to shit before you get to the airport or hit the highway. If you are flying, your pooping woes will start at the security lines, and won't end until you are safely settled at your destination. Avoid unnecessary stress by packing well in advance. Arrive at the airport early, fully nourished, and with your favorite music or a good book, like this one. Drink a lot of water before, during, and after your flight to fight dehydration and jetlag. Bring along plenty of healthy snacks to munch on so you'll are less tempted to eat processed junk food. For long flights you may opt for an aisle seat so you can easily access the potty—since you will be drinking

Chapter 4: Going Public

more fluids—and also give you body and your bowels some much need stretches and movement.

The poop clock

Even if you poop at regular times at home, you may find that hopping a lot of time zones throws your poop clock way off. There are loads of techniques and apps to minimize jetlag and ease into your new time zone. Give them a go to get your poops and your sleep patterns back on track quickly.

Vacation Dining

You certainly should be allowed to indulge yourself while on vacation. But loading up on foods with lots of fat, sugar and salt will also load you up with a lot of constipation. Between binges seek out some healthy high-fiber entrees to help offset some intestinal stress. And as was covered before, drink plenty of water—especially when partying with booze—for better shits and smaller hangovers.

Get off your ass

Your exercise routine—if you even have one—can easily go out the window when you travel, and that of course can mess up your turd flow. Even if you can't or won't want to visit the hotel gym, going for a daily walk or swim can certainly improve your turd frequency.

Final note

If all else fails, the final travel tip is to pack along some fiber tablets to help keep you regular. That way, if your shits are not cooperating, or if you decide to just eat like shit and lay around the pool the whole time, you will at least have a shot at having regular poops. Happy travels!

World Toilets

The traditional porcelain toilet that you are used to shitting on can be found in many developed countries where westerners live or travel. Some countries, such as Japan, have raised the bar for pooping and turned the lowly toilet into a high-tech luxury device. If you visit there, your ass might have the good fortune of encountering an automatic bidet. These popular, toilet gadgets will do everything except take a shit for you. They warm, spray, and dry your ass at the touch of a few buttons. If you fall in love with one of these technological wonders, you can buy and install one on your toilet at home.

Squat Toilets

If you travel outside the US, particularly to Asia, you may encounter toilets that are essentially just a porcelain hole in the floor. These squat toilets—however unusual for you—do not need to be a

Chapter 4: Going Public

terrifying experience. You will do well to prepare in advance so you can more easily navigate these setups.

Set into the floor, a squat toilet is usually a pair of porcelain foot pads astride a shallow bowl that has a toilet drain in the middle. The good news is that you will have an ergonomically optimal pooping posture without having to make contact with a toilet seat. The bad news, however, is that it can be difficult to balance and navigate with your clothes on—so you may elect to strip below your waist and try to keep your feet flat on the ground.

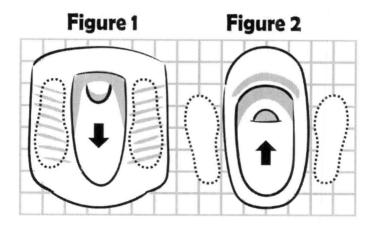

There are three variations of these toilets. The first version (fig. 1) usually has the drain hole on one end. Simply place your ass over the hole and go. The

Have a Great Shit

second version (fig. 2) has a small half-domed splash guard at one end. In this version you want to face the guard and pee towards it when you are shitting. The third version looks like a standard western toilet, except the bowl has foot pads (like fig. 1) for you to stand on. Just climb atop the bowl, squat down, and get to it!

Depending on the setup, squatters are often accompanied by a trash can, a bucket or trough of water, and a ladle or cup. An important thing to note is that squat toilets don't usually have TP or hand soap, so for best results bring some in your Shit Kit. The plumbing for a squat toilet is not always equipped to handle toilet paper, so wrap up your TP and dispose of it in the trash can. If you end up without any TP, make like a local and use the provided cup to splash upwards and wash your butt crack clean. In countries with squat toilets, it is common for people to only wipe and clean their butts with their left hands, and only touch food or shake hands with the right hand—for obvious sanitation reasons.

Operating a squat toilet can also be a little strange when compared to a Western flushing throne. Depending on where you are, there may be no flush handle. This is where the bucket and ladle come in. Use the cup to pour water into the toilet and it will

Chapter 4: Going Public

flush the contents. You then pour some water around the toilet and foot pads to clean them if needed. This explains why the floor is sometimes wet, not from piss, but from the water.

If squat toilets sound horrifying, it might help to remember that billions of people don't even have that luxury. They have to shit in an open hole, or in a bucket, or out in a field. You may also be relieved to find that squat restrooms usually do not smell any worse than traditional restrooms.

There are many travel websites and guide books that have good tips for using the local toilets where you will be travelling to—read up and be prepared before you go.

Drop Anchor

If you ever have to 'hit the head' (use the toilet) on a small ship at sea, you may find that it requires a bit more manual labor than a land-based crapper. The head is a small toilet that usually has a dial and a pump handle off to one side. After you are done doing your business, move the dial to the flush position and begin pumping. This flushes the bowl's contents it into the ship's holding tank. When that is done, you switch the dial back and pump some water back into the bowl for the next shipmate to poop (or if they are seasick) barf into.

Zero Gravity

No book on pooping would be complete without mentioning how to poop in space—since that is apparently where we will all be living in just a few short years. It is advisable to ask a fellow crew member to show you the ropes, but if you weren't paying attention during astronaut training and are too embarrassed to ask, I will do my best to walk you through it.

Chapter 4: Going Public

On the ISS (International Space Station) you will notice that the toilet is fairly small, because zero gravity doesn't really allow you to sit on it. Instead, you will essentially end up floating and shitting over a 19 million dollar vacuum shit-box. First you put a new collection bag in the toilet. Then you strap your feet in to the restraints, so you don't go floating off the pot. Finally, to keep your shits from freely moving about the cabin, carefully aim your butt over the 4" hole, flip the suction lever and fire away. That is how you hurl a turd in zero gravity!

Have a Great Shit

Chapter 5

Don't be a Shit

There are a few golden rules to follow when you use a public or shared bathroom. When observed, these courtesies will ensure that everyone has a more pleasant experience, and will prevent you from accidentally being an ass.

Stall Manners

The first unwritten social rule in a public bathroom is to select a stall away from any other occupied potties (this rule applies to urinals as well). A quick glance on your way in to the bathroom, will usually reveal a stall that is absent of feet. If the stall door is closed, the next courtesy to follow is to err on the side of caution by knocking first and then waiting a second, rather than barging in. Also bear in mind that only creeps poke their head under the stall door to check.

Once you settle in, do your best to refrain from conversation so everyone can focus on their own shit. Catch up with your buddies outside afterwards. The bathroom is also a poor location for loitering, eating lunch, or conducting business, so don't answer your phone or bring in work unless you are a plumber fixing the toilet. Instead, use the quiet time to relax without distraction for a moment and think of some pleasant thoughts. Finally, let us all resist the urge to laugh or comment on loud or strange noises, especially our own.

Pay it Forward

Once your deed is done at a public potty, it is time to do your part so that the next patron doesn't get an awful surprise behind door number three. Put the seat back down, wipe it off, and make sure to flush all of the bowl's contents. You will also be awarded karma points if you leave the stall door open so that no one has to play the guessing game. A final act of kindness is to report an absence of TP or other lavatorial mishaps to someone in charge.

Guest Bathroom

The best piece of advice when using someone else's bathroom is to leave it the way you found it. Wipe up any water around the sink, and keep it classy by putting the lid and seat down, and don't be a shit and leave shit or skid marks in the bowl. Hopefully your host has provided a hand towel or two, but if not you

Chapter 5: Don't be a Shit

can shake your hands dry, wipe them on your pants, or lightly use the side of a bath towel—but only if your hands are REALLY clean.

As a side note, some of you may be tempted to sneak a little peak to see what's in your host's medicine cabinet. I implore you to refrain from the perversion and allow your guests their privacy. Besides, it is best to leave unwarranted snooping to the government.

Shit Heads

I think we can agree that anyone who vandalizes a public bathroom, by scrawling stupid shit on the walls, or damaging the fixtures is a shit head. Public potties deserve respect for the truly wonderful convenience that they offer. These facilities cost money to build and maintain, yet they are often provided for free! Let us not forget that we owe a debt of gratitude to the poor under-paid employee who has to go in and clean up after the countless slobs who dirty up the place. So let's all do our part by treating public bathrooms with the respect and reverence they deserve.

Have a Great Shit

Chapter 6

The Perfect Potty

Hopefully by now you have a newfound appreciation for the importance of a good shit. And I hope I can make a convincing argument that the place where you shit most deserves some special attention. While it may not seem like an overly-important part of your dwelling, the average person visits the bathroom 2,500 times a year and will spend 2 to 3 years of their life courting the toilet. The atmosphere your create and accessories your furnish can provide a relaxing and comfortable environment in which to do your business.

Bathroom Basics - Supplies

A bathroom well-stocked, with essential cleaning and pooping accessories, will ensure that you and your guests are prepared to deal with any surprises or inconveniences that may occur.

Toilet paper

There is no rule when it comes to what type of toilet paper you should buy. You will likely be confronted

Have a Great Shit

with a myriad of options such as sheet thickness, eco-friendliness, chemical-free, sheet count, softness, and strength to name a few. If you are a value-hunter, it is easiest to compare packages by the total square feet or the total number of sheets, rather than the number of rolls.

For storage, be sure to put your extra rolls of TP near the toilet so when you run out mid-wipe you can easily access a fresh roll. You can also purchase a standalone caddy if you don't have a nearby cabinet to stash your rolls.

Once home, you will be confronted with a critical TP choice: which way to mount it. There are few topics more polarizing than how to 'correctly' install a new roll of toilet paper.

On the one hand you have the 'over' camp who will staunchly defend how their method makes it easier to

Chapter 6: The Perfect Potty

grab hold of. Then you have the 'under' crowd who are quick to point out how their preference prevents accidental unwinding caused by kiddies, kitties, and the occasional sloppy yank.

So who is right? Whoever puts on the fresh roll, or whoever cares the most. Just don't let your preference in toilet paper direction end your marriage.

Plunger

These life-saving devices are a must-have for those times when the toilet water heads in the wrong direction. A sink plunger—which usually has a red rubber cup at the end—is what most people think of for uncloggirg a toilet. As its name indicates, this not actually the right tool for the job.

PLUNGERS 101

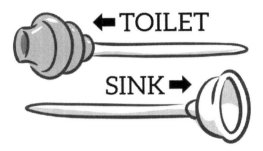

The preferred type—a toilet plunger (or flange plunger)—has a specialized black cup which makes a nice seal and won't slide around and make a mess like the sink plunger.

Since plungers are usually kind of ugly, and ideally used infrequently, they can be kept out of sight or in the garage. There are also fancy plunger-holders that conceal the cup for a nicer aesthetic.

Toilet brush

What better way to combat skid marks than with a giant wiry toilet toothbrush? Have it near the shitter so you can scrub them shits off while they are still fresh. Of course since toilet brushes are not the most

Chapter 6: The Perfect Potty

pleasant of bathroom accessories, you want to find one with an enclosed base that conceals the brush when you are done using it. And don't be afraid to replace it when it starts looking really scary.

Hand towels

Unless you like the thought of your guests using your personal bath towel to dry their hands after shitting, you may want to invest in some hand towels to hang by the sink. Look for plush towels, which are extra absorbent and have a nice soft touch. Also, having several mears that you can swap in a few fresh ones between loads of laundry.

Tissues

Keeping a box of facial tissues near the toilet can be both a convenience and a life-saver. If you need to blow your nose in the bathroom, facial tissue is less abrasive and holds up better than toilet paper. Conversely, if you run out of TP, then the tissue can double as emergency toilet paper.

Hand Soap

Hopefully you are sold on the idea of washing your hands with soap and water after using the toilet. If so, encourage everyone to wash up by having a soap dispenser at the sink. Liquid soap is easier to dispense and can be a bit more pleasant than a slimy bar that everyone has been rubbing with their hands.

Toilet cleaner

If you give a shit about the cleanliness and appearance of your toilet, you likely already have the cleaning supplies needed to get the job done. If, however, you'd like to give this new and interesting concept a try, here are some tips to get you started. Cleaning your toilet bowl once a week keeps stains and smells at bay, and the best way to do it is with a toilet brush and some toilet cleaner. Just squirt some cleaner under the bowl rim, let it sit, scrub it, and flush. If you are an environmental-type and don't like the harsh chemicals found in many commercial toilet cleaners, or if you just like to save some money, you can sprinkle in some baking soda and distilled white vinegar to make a fizzy, all-natural cleaner. It is also advisable to have a pair of dedicated cleaning gloves or sponges that are only used for scrubbing the crapper.

Calming Commodes

Part of what makes a good shit go well is to be relaxed when you are on the pot. You are more likely to loosen up and squeeze one out if you are in a relaxed setting. So why not make your restroom a room of

Chapter 6: The Perfect Potty

rest? It may be worth the effort to turn that sterile shit-box into a welcoming sanctuary. You will also make a good impression with your guests, or your date, by letting them know that you have your priorities straight.

Lighting

One easy way to change the vibe of a bathroom (or any room for that matter) from feeling cold and crappy, to warm and relaxing, is to replace the light bulbs with warmer color temperature bulbs. People generally find warm, yellow lights (like a candle flame) to be more calming, and cold blue lights (like daylight and fluorescents) to be less-calming. Pick bulbs with a color temperature rating between 2,700K-3,300K.

If you have cooler 3,500K-4,500K incandescent bulbs, you can create a mellower vibe by putting them on a dimmer. Plugging in a nightlight will make it easier to find the light switch in the dark or otherwise allow you to pretend that you are shitting by moonlight.

Toilet mats

If the bathroom floor makes your feet cold when you are on the pot, your body—and your booty—will not be fully relaxed for a nice turd release. If you easily get cold feet or just want a cushy foot pad, throw a bath mat in front of the toilet.

Have a Great Shit

Aroma

Pleasant fragrances can make the bathroom a more enjoyable place to visit, so long as the scents are not overwhelming. Just remember that what may smell good to you may be totally repulsive to others. Candles, incense, or dried flower sachets are just a few items you can place near the toilet. Vanilla or sandalwood scents are usually considered mild and pleasant. Some people swear by using toilet sprays in the toilet before they poop. See Chapter 1 for tips on buying or making your own spray to help cover up those stinkers.

Bidet seats

To really experience luxury shitting, you can drop some coin on a fancy-ass automatic bidet seat. As previously mentioned, some of the swanky models come with cushioned, heated seats, music players, and a fan to dry your butt. The heated seats might also relax your derrière so much that it brings on the urge for a number two, even if you were only planning on a quick tinkle.

Decorate

How you decorate your bathroom is of course entirely up to you. If you are at a total loss for ideas, look online or in home decoration magazines for

Chapter 6: The Perfect Potty

suggestions or examples. When done right, wall colors, accents, and artwork can all give your bathroom a classy and chill vibe. And if you opt to stock your potty with some reading material, I might suggest a copy of this book.

Have a Great Shit

Chapter 7

Potty Humor

A book about shit and shitting would not be complete without a selection of poop jokes and commonly-used phrases to describe the act. These can also come in handy for those times when you are looking to surprise or dazzle your friends—no matter how proper you think they are.

Shitty Jokes

A man visits his doctor and explains that he regularly poops at 8 o'clock every morning. The doctor says, "That's great, what's the problem?" The man replies, "I don't wake up until 9."

Why are most people like laxatives? They irritate the shit out of you.

Politicians are like diapers. They should be changed frequently and for the same reason.

Q: Why did the toilet paper roll down the hill?
A: To get to the bottom

Have a Great Shit

A bear and a rabbit are pooping in the woods one day. The bear asks the rabbit, "Hey Rabbit, do you ever have problems with poop sticking to your fur?" The rabbit finishes his poop and replies "No, I don't". "That's great!" says the bear as he promptly wipes his butt with the rabbit.

Q: Did you hear about the movie Constipation?
A: It never came out.

Q: Did you hear about the sequel, Diarrhea?
A: It got bad reviews so they had to release it early.

Chapter 7: Potty Humor

Farting in an elevator is simply wrong on so many levels.

You are on the bus when you suddenly realize that you need to fart. The music is really loud, so you time your farts with the beat. After a couple of songs, you start to feel better. When you get up to exit at your stop you notice that all the people are staring at you, and that's when you remember: you've been listening with your earbuds.

Farts are like children. The only ones you can stand are your own.

The Shit List

The Phantom Shit

You are pretty sure you shit, but when you turn around and check the bowl, there is no sign of a turd.

The Non-Stick Shit

These shits are so slick and easy that you don't even feel them on the way out. There is nothing on the toilet paper and you have to look in the bowl to be sure you actually went.

The No Shit Shit

You sit on the pot for a while and only fart a few times.

Full Retreat

You have to shit but don't take the opportunity to go. Then your turd decides to go back into hiding for a long time.

Partial Retreat

You are able to hold your shit at bay the first time, but you better find a toilet fast, because you may not be so lucky the second time.

Chapter 7: Potty Humor

The U-Turn Shit

You already finished wiping, and are headed to wash your hand, when you realize that you still have a partial load to excavate.

Belt Hole Shit

You shit so much that you probably dropped a whole pant size.

The Run-For-It Shit!

You have 10 seconds to find a toilet or your are going to need to change your pants!

Shy Shit

This shit takes a peek outside and decides go back into hiding.

The Big Fart

You think you are going to have a really good shit, but it just turns out to be a giant fart. False alarm.

The Piece of Shit

This piece of shit refuses to be flushed no matter how many times you push the handle—especially if you are out in public or at a party.

Have a Great Shit

The (Colonel) Clinger
This stubborn shit has made its exit but has separation anxiety and refuses get in the toilet.

The Shit! Shit
When you run out of TP half way through cleanup.

The Forever Shit
The kind of shit that that takes half an hour just to get 1/3 of the way out.

The Cannonball Shit
A shit that makes a big splash on exit and soaks your butt.

Chapter 8

Talking Shit

The word 'shit' is one of the most versatile tools in the English language. It can be used as a noun, a verb, or an adjective. When used in common expressions it can mean anything from extremely good to extremely bad, which is why you must take care when adding it your lexicon. Calling someone 'the shit' versus 'a shit' could mean the difference between paying your respects or getting your ass kicked. Following are some of the more popular 'shit' phrases and their respective meanings.

Positive expressions

Take a shit

The act of pooping. When something breaks.

The shit

A person, thing, or event held in high regard.

Good shit

A consumable item of high quality.

Have a Great Shit

Knowing your shit
To be knowledgeable about a particular subject.

Shooting the shit
Idly chatting about unimportant topics.

I shit you not
To let someone know you are being honest.

Mixed expressions

Give a shit
To care about something or someone. Can also be used ironically to show that you don't care.

...and shit
A filler phrase used at the end of a list or sentence.

Your Shit / my shit
Usually a reference for possessions.

Shit faced
To be very drunk.

Holy shit
A non-religious expression to show shock or surprise.

Chapter 8: Talking Shit

Negative expressions

Shit

Slang for feces or poop. Also used to describe a person, place, or thing, of little value.

Shit head

Someone who acts selfishly without regard for others.

Piece of shit

A person of bad character or a defective item.

Full of shit/Bullshitter

A person who lies or exaggerates.

Shit sandwich

An undesirable or chaotic situation.

Give shit

To tease, insult, or harass someone.

Bullshit

To mislead someone or express frustration.

Get your shit together

To bring order to your personal belongings or your life's situation.

Have a Great Shit

Scare the shit out of someone
Excessively frightening someone

Scared shitless / shit a brick
The act of being excessively frightened.

Deep Shit
When you are in a lot of trouble.

Up shit creek
See: Deep shit

Shit-can
To throw something away or fire someone from a job.

No shit?!
Shows that you are impressed, or used ironically to imply that a statement was obvious.

Not give a shit
To not care at all.

Tough shit
Shows a lack of sympathy in a situation.

Chapter 8: Talking Shit

Shit happens

A phrase that implies that bad things sometimes happen for no reason.

Shit for brains

Someone who acts unintelligently.

A shit list

a mental list of people with whom you have a grudge or dislike.

When the shit hits the fan

An event that does or will cause significant trouble.

Does a bear shit in the woods?

A rhetorical question said in response to an obvious question where the answer would be 'yes'.

Shit or get off the pot/can

Telling someone they need to make a decision without further deliberation.

Shit out of luck / S.O.L.

No good options are left. The situation is without luck.

Shit Happens

Using humorous phrases to allude to the act of pooping has long been a tradition between friends (usually male). Below are some of the very best for your enjoyment. The next time you go to excuse yourself for the restroom, you can impress your friends with one of these charming phrases—or better yet come up with one of your own!

"Excuse me, I've got to..."

Answer the call of the wild
Audit my Assets
Bake some brownies
Bomb the bowl
Build a bench
Bury an elf
Chop a log
Clean the tuba
Commune with nature
Conduct a movement
Cook a burrito
Cut some rope
Dispose of some hazardous waste
Do the Royal Squat
Drop a bomb

Chapter 8: Talking Shit

Dump a load
Feed the fish
Fire the cannon
Float a boat
Force the duck to quack
Give a burial at sea
Have a shit
Heave a Havana
Help the groundhog find his shadow
Hurl a turd
Inspect the facilities
Launch a torpedo
Lay some cable
Let my people go
Lose some weight the quick way
Make a deposit at the porcelain bank
Make a log entry
Off-load some freight
Park some bark
Pass the baton
Pay the plumber
Peel the wallpaper
Pinch a loaf
Release the hounds
Ride the hoop
Roll a nut log
Send a message to the White House
Sink the Bismarck

Have a Great Shit

Squeeze a coily
Take a dump
Take the kids to the water slide
Test the plumbing
Update the Captain's log
Yodel in the canyon

Chapter 8: Talking Shit

Bathroom Terms	**Poop Terms**
Can	Bowel movement (or BM)
Chamber Pot	Business
Commode	Crap
Crapper	Defecation
Dunny	Do-do
Facilities	Doodie
Head	Dookie
John	Dump
Latrine	Dung
Lavatory	Evacuation
Loo	Excrement
Outhouse	Feces
Oval Office	Load
Pot	Loaf
Potty	Log
Powder room	Number Two
Privy	Pile
Reading Room	Plop
Restroom	Poo
Shitter	Poop
Thunder Mug	Poopie
Thunder Box	Poopoo
Throne	Shit
Toilet	Steamer
Wash room	Stool
Water Closet (W.C.)	Turd

Have a Great Shit

Chapter 9

Interesting Shit

Here are a few more tidbits of trivia for you to digest and enjoy.

Toilets

Mark your calendars; World Toilet Day is celebrated on November 19th, and National Poop Day is celebrated on the day after the Super Bowl.

We pay homage to the toilet an average of 2,500 times per year, which adds up to about 3 years of your life spent in the bathroom.

It is believed that as an employee of Thomas Crapper, Arthur Giblin invented the first flushable toilet. Giblin purportedly sold the patent to Crapper who then made the invention famous. To this day Crapper's family enjoys the honor of being a slang term for defecation.

More toilets flush during halftime of football's Big Game than at any other time of year.

Have a Great Shit

It is estimated that 40,000 people in the U.S. are injured on toilets each year, which is also on par with a similar number of annual golf injuries.

The average person uses 21,000 sheets of toilet paper a year (about 23 football fields).

60% of the people on earth do not have access to a flush toilet or good sanitation.

Turds

Your poop is 75% water. The solid mass consists of 30% dead bacteria, 10% fats, 10% inorganic material, and 2% protein.

The average turd weighs 1 lb.

Parcopresis is a condition in which a person cannot shit at all if anyone is nearby.

There are four bags of Neil Armstrong's dookie on the moon.

Parents will change a baby's diapers about 10,000 times.

Biogas from poop is being converted into electric energy at various sewage plants around the world.

Chapter 9: Interesting Shit

The world's longest recorded turd was 26 feet.

The smell of books gives some people the urge to shit—dubbed the Mariko Aoki phenomenon.

The term 'Shit happens' is first credited to Carl Werthman in 1964

Fecal transplants are a method of placing shit from a healthy person into the colon of a sick person to restore beneficial bacteria colonies.

The Gut

The gut is the only organ in the body that can do its duties without the brain.

Your digestive tract is essentially a 30-foot long tube that starts at your mouth and ends at your butt.

60-80% of your immune system cells are in your gut

One study showed that gut bacteria possibly plays a major role in obesity, cancer, depression, and anxiety.

The surface area of your small intestine is roughly 2,700 square feet

Have a Great Shit

Your tummy can defy gravity and digest your food even when you are upside down.

The digestive system is the most likely organ to cause death from cancer.

The small intestine absorbs the nutrients from your food and passes it into your bloodstream.

The large intestine is only 5 feet in length, while the small intestine is an impressive 15-20 feet.

You can survive without a large intestine (but you turds will be really watery).

Farts

People fart an average of 14 times a day.

Only 1 % of your fart cloud is stinky.

A fart travels at 7 mph.

The SBD ('Silent but deadly') variety of farts are the result of bacteria and fermentation that release methane and sulphur in your gut—which is why it smells more. Since the amount of foul air produced is of a lower volume, it slips through quietly. This also

Chapter 9: Interesting Shit

makes it more difficult to identify y the perpetrator in a public setting.

Loud farts are usually caused from swallowing air or soda carbonation. They make more noise since there is a larger volume of air trying to get out of your butt (just like a whoopee cushion). Because these farts are mostly carbon dioxide & oxygen, they usually don't smell as bad.

Farts are flammable, but lighting them is hazardous to your ass.

Research shows that couples who can freely fart in front of each other tend to stay together longer.

Have a Great Shit

The (rear) End

Congratulations, you made it to the end of the book! I certainly hope you had fun learning about all of this shit. This is my first book so I invite you to send any comments, questions, ideas, praises, or helpful heckles.

Be well & shit well!

Warmly,
Jesse Karras

email: jesse@haveagreatshit.com
facebook, instagram & twitter: haveagreatshit

Gift a copy and leave a nice review on Amazon!

Made in the USA
Middletown, DE
11 December 2023